Notes for parents and teachers

Life-Cycle Books have been specially written and designed
to provide a simple, yet informative, series of factual
nature books for young children.
The illustrations are bright and clear, and children can
'read' the pictures while the story is read to them. However,
the text has been specially set in large type to make it easy
for children to follow or to read for themselves.

They cannot see very well,
and rely on being able to
hear and smell instead.

Hedgehogs feed mainly at night, shuffling along with their noses to the ground sniffing out insects, slugs and other small animals.

If they catch a worm
they will run backwards with it,
to pull it free from its hole.

They also like fruit and
some vegetables and will eat
bread and milk if it is offered.

In Spring a male hedgehog
will seek a female.
When they first meet she will
probably bite or kick him.
He then walks round and
round her, courting her with
spitting and hissing noises!

They meet nose to nose and
sniff one another.
Again she may bite him.
It can take some hours before
she will allow him to mate.

After mating, the female will
make a nursery nest which
she lines with grass.
Her young will be born
in about five weeks.

At birth the baby hedgehogs'
spines are covered with skin
so they don't hurt their mother.
Very soon their soft white spines
push through this skin.

The baby hedgehogs suckle
milk from their mother and
grow very fast.

When their mother leaves the nest
in search of a meal for herself
she covers her babies with
grass and leaves to keep
them safe.

If the nest is disturbed, perhaps
by smoke from a bonfire, or
by a stoat or fox, she will
carry her babies to a new nest.

After a couple of weeks the
young hedgehogs' eyes open.
By this time their hard
brown spines are growing too.

Soon they learn to roll into
a ball when danger threatens.
Later they will also learn to
get up on their legs and run.

When their adult spines have
started to grow, their mother
takes them out in search of food.
If one strays too far from her and
gets frightened it will whistle.
The mother hurries over to
lead it back to the others.

When the young have finished
suckling milk from their mother
they will start to wander
farther away from home.
Soon they will leave
to live on their own.

Foxes, badgers and stoats will
attack and eat young hedgehogs,
or even older ones that are sleeping.
But the hedgehogs' worst enemies
are cars and lorries.
Many hedgehogs get run over
when crossing the road.

Hedgehogs can climb trees and
walls and will curl into a ball
to fall down the other side.
They can also swim if they need to.

Hedgehogs are covered in
fleas, mites and other small animals.
One hedgehog may have more
than five hundred fleas on it!

They can use their hind legs to
scratch between their spines
and behind their ears.

Sometimes hedgehogs make
a liquid foam in their mouths
which they put on their spines.
It is called 'anointing' and
some people think they may
do it to get rid of the animals
living on them.

In Autumn hedgehogs eat
lots of extra food and
get very fat. This helps them
to survive the winter.
They make themselves warm nests
of leaves to sleep in during
the cold weather.

They may wake up on
warmer nights and go in
search of more food.
They return home to sleep again
until Spring arrives.

When the warm weather returns
they will be out looking for
a mate to start a new family.

LONGMAN GROUP LIMITED
Longman House
Burnt Mill, Harlow, Essex CM20 2JE, England
and Associated Companies throughout the World.

© Althea Braithwaite 1985
All rights reserved; no part of this publication
may be reproduced, stored in a retrieval system,
or transmitted in any form or by any means, electronic,
mechanical, photocopying, recording or otherwise,
without the prior written permission of the Publishers.

First published 1985
Second impression 1986

ISBN 0 582 25259 8 (pbk edition)
ISBN 0 582 25264 4 (csd edition)

Set in 'Monophoto' Plantin 18/24 pt

Produced by Longman Group (FE) Ltd
Printed in Hong Kong